I AM NOT ALONE
I STILL MATTER

To the unhoused reader,
this book is for you

DR. ABRAHAM KHOUREIS, Ph.D.
The Apostle of Compassionate Leadership

Copyright Notice

Copyright © 2025 by Dr. Abraham Khoureis. All Rights Reserved.

No part of this publication, including but not limited to "I Am Not Alone. I Still Matter," may be reproduced, stored in a database or retrieval system, or distributed, or transmitted in any form or by any means, including photocopying, recording, or other electronic or mechanical methods, without the prior written permission of the copyright holder, except in the case of brief quotations embodied in critical reviews and certain other noncommercial uses permitted by copyright law. For permission requests, write to the copyright holder at the address below.

ANG POWER PUBLISHING HOUSE
PO BOX 10735 / Glendale, CA 91209-USA
ANGPowerPHouse@Gmail.com
ISBN: 978-1-966837-23-7

This publication contains proprietary information pertaining to "I Am Not Alone. I Still Matter." Unauthorized use, duplication, or adaptation of the concepts, graphics, or other materials within is strictly prohibited and punishable under applicable laws.

Disclaimer: The author and publisher have made every effort to ensure the accuracy of the information in this publication. However, they assume no responsibility for errors or omissions or for any consequences resulting from the use of the information provided. This book is intended for educational and informational purposes only and does not constitute professional or legal advice.

All trademarks, service marks, product names, and logos referenced in this book are the property of their respective owners. Insights provided in "I Am Not Alone. I Still Matter," are the intellectual property of Dr. Abraham Khoureis and are protected under copyright law.

First Edition - Printed in the United States of America

"Homelessness is not the absence of a home, it is the absence of safety, belonging, and being seen. Every unhoused soul is a productive life interrupted."
Dr. Abraham Khoureis

This page intentionally left blank for your initial reading reflection

Copyright © 2025 by Dr. Abraham Khoureis. All Rights Reserved.

Table of Contents

Preface 1
Let's Begin Together 3
You Are Not Alone 5
Reclaiming Your Dignity 11
Daily Mindset Tools 19
Mental Health While Homeless 25
Addiction and Recovery 33
Staying Safe on the Streets 37
Faith, Spirituality, or Inner Strength 41
How to Rebuild Relationships 44
Navigating the System 49
Where to Go for Help 53
Small Jobs, Big Steps 57
Stories of People Who Made It 61
Journaling Pages or Prompts 67
What to Say to Yourself Every Day 70
A Directory of Love 73
When You Help Some Else You Heal Too 78
A Note from Someone Who Cares 81
Other Books by Dr. Abraham Khoureis, Ph.D. 85

This page intentionally left blank for your initial reading reflection

Copyright © 2025 by Dr. Abraham Khoureis. All Rights Reserved.

Dedication

To every unhoused soul who ever felt invisible, this book is a reminder from the world that you are seen. You are visible. You are worthy, and you are not alone.

May this book bring you hope, strength, and a loud reminder that your life story still matter.

For those unhoused beautiful souls who I interviewed for the background story for this book, thank you for sharing your life story of sacrifices, survival, recovery, and triumph of rejoining back our society.

This book is for you.

This page intentionally left blank for your initial reading reflection

Copyright © 2025 by Dr. Abraham Khoureis. All Rights Reserved.

Preface

This book was not written for the world that forgot you. It was written exclusively for you.

For the soul who is still breathing through pain, sleeping with one eye open, eating when you can, and surviving when no one is watching. I do not know your name, your full story, or how you came to be where you are, but I do know this: you are still here. And that means something.

You are not invisible. No matter how far life has taken you from where you once stood, there is still a path that leads forward. A real one. One with steps you can take, slowly, imperfectly, and bravely.

This book is not a lecture. It is not here to judge you, blame you, shame you, or pretend it knows your exact pain. It is here to just walk beside you. Quietly, kindly, and without conditions.

Inside these pages are truths, tools, and resources. There are reflections to help you see your own strength. There are words meant to remind you of something sacred: You Are Not Alone. You Still Matter. Repeat after me:

I Am Not Alone. I Still Matter.

If you hold this book in your hands, I hope you feel that someone believes in you. Many others do, and I am not the only one.

Let's Begin Together

Homelessness is not just about lacking shelter. It's about carrying a weight no one sees. The weight of being looked through. Of feeling disposable. Of being told, with eyes or silence, that you are no longer part of the world and society that once welcomed you.

But here is something no one tells you enough: if you have made it this far, you are already strong. Not the kind of strength that always looks good, but the kind that keeps going through rain, rejection, cold nights, and lonely mornings.

This book was created to give you something no one can take away, knowledge, belief, and direction.

You will find:

- Pages to help you shift your mindset when the world feels too heavy
- Practical steps to stay safe, fed, and connected

- Ways to deal with addiction, trauma, and deep pain without shame
- True stories from people who've walked through the fire and found their way back
- Resources, actual places, programs, and services that want to help you
- Messages that speak to the part of you the world forgot: your humanity

You do not have to read it all at once. Start anywhere. Skip what you do not need. Come back to what you do. Tear a page out and keep it in your pocket. This book is yours, and it will never look down on you.

You are not just trying to survive homelessness. You are learning to survive a world that made it so easy to lose everything, and that is a fight few understand.

    So, turn the page. Let's begin together.

You Are Not Alone

Let us begin with the one thing you may not have heard in a long time: **You are not alone. You Still Matter.**

I know it might not feel that way.

When people pass you like you are not there… When a cold night feels like it might never end… When you are sitting in a shelter full of strangers and yet feel completely unseen…

It is easy to believe no one cares.
It is easy to believe You are invisible.

Here is the truth you need to know, many do care about you, and I am just a humble one of them. You are holding this book because someone, somewhere, believed in your life enough to put these pages in your hands. That belief is real. Now, it is yours to carry.

Being unhoused, unsheltered, displaced, whatever word you use, it is not just about not having a roof. It is about the emotional weight. The silence. The loneliness that creeps in and tries to convince you are no longer part of the world.

But you are.

You still have a place here.

You are not broken beyond repair. You are not forgotten.

There are others like you, right now, wondering if they matter. There are people sleeping in cars who never thought they would end up there. There are mothers keeping their kids warm with blankets and prayers. There are young people who ran away because it was safer to run. There are elders who gave everything, only to be left with nothing. They are not less than. You are not less than. You are human. You carry worth that no circumstance can erase.

If you have lost family, if your friends stopped answering, if no one checks on you anymore, please do not take that as proof you do not matter. Pain convinces us of lies. But your pain is not your identity. You are more than what's happened to you.

Let this book be the beginning of a new voice in your life.
One that speaks truth back to the lies. One that reminds you, every step of the way, you are not walking this alone.

If you can, let yourself look around, not just to survive, but to connect. Say hello to someone near you. Offer a smile if it feels right. Ask someone where they're from, or how they're doing, or where they found shelter last night.
Build a thread of belonging. Even a small one. That's where hope grows. You do not have to do everything at once. Just hold this one truth close:

You are not alone. Not now. Not anymore.

When everything falls apart, the first thing we often lose is not money or shelter, it is connection. People pass by without looking. Friends disappear. Family may give up, or maybe they were never there to begin with. It's easy to start believing the lie that you are utterly, completely alone. But you are not.

Right now, somewhere in this world, someone else is sitting on a bench wondering how they got here. Someone is sleeping in their car with a blanket across the dashboard for privacy. Someone is staring at the sky from a shelter cot, trying to remember what hope used to feel like. Someone, maybe you, is reading this book and wondering if they even deserve to.

Let me say it clearly: **You do.**

You deserve to be reminded of your dignity, no matter what your circumstances look like right now. Being homeless does not erase your past, your value, or your right to the future. You are not the sum of your mistakes, your losses, or the judgments of people who've never walked in your shoes.

The world may not make space for you easily. But this page does. This book does. I do.

What Loneliness Tells You, and Why It Lies?

Loneliness whispers terrible things:

"That no one cares."
"That you'll never get out."
"That you have failed."

Loneliness is not always telling the truth; it is telling the pain. Pain does not see clearly. It exaggerates, repeats, and tries to convince you that this moment will never end.

But it will.

If you have felt invisible, know that I see you. If you have felt abandoned, know that this book was written because someone refused to abandon the idea of you.

There Are Others

There are volunteers handing out food who once stood in line themselves. There are outreach workers who were once addicted, arrested, or living on sidewalks. There are quiet souls in libraries, churches, bus stations, and public parks who are watching, wondering, hurting, just like you.

You are not the only one. That is not to minimize your pain, it is to remind you that you are part of a story bigger than your current struggle. That you are not strange, cursed, or forgotten, and you are not alone.

There Are Many People Who Still Care

- You may not have met them yet. But they exist.
- A nurse who does not look away.
- A stranger who says hello without judgment.
- A shelter worker who smiles like it matters.
- A reader of this book who may pass it on to someone else.

Caring still exists. And sometimes, it comes when we stop expecting it. Sometimes it arrives in the form of a book like this one. A small act. A quiet voice. A moment of light.

Let this be one of those moments. You are not alone. Even if no one has said it lately.
Even if no one says it again tomorrow. Let this page say it today, and let it be enough, for now.

Reclaiming Your Dignity

You may have lost a lot, but you have not lost your dignity. Even if people treat you like you have. Even if the mirror does not feel like a friend anymore. Even if your head stays low and your eyes avoid others. The truth is, no one can take your dignity from you. Only you can lay it down. And today might be the day you start picking it back up.

Dignity is not about what you wear or where you live. It's not about having a title, a paycheck, or a clean past. It's deeper than that. It is the quiet belief that your life still matters, without needing anyone to confirm it.

You can reclaim your dignity even on the hardest days.

You do it when you make your bed in a shelter or on the ground. You do it when you say "no" to something that does not feel right.

You do it when you hold on to your values, even when no one is watching. You do it when you choose kindness over bitterness, even if just for a moment. You do it when you look someone in the eye and refuse to shrink.

Maybe you have done things you are not proud of. Maybe life broke you in places you are still learning how to name. But your mistakes do not define your worth. And neither does your suffering.

Dignity is quiet. It does not yell for attention. It does not need applause. It just stands back up. Even when it is tired. Even when it's hurting. Even when no one's looking. If you have been made to feel like a burden, let me say this clearly: You are not a burden. You are a blessing.

You carry memory, soul, love, humor, wisdom, and potential. Even if they are buried right now, they are still in you. And if others do not see your dignity yet, that is their blindness, not your failure.

So today, try something small. Wash your face with care. Fold your blanket neatly.

Speak to yourself without insult.

Stand with your shoulders back.

Tell yourself, "I'm still me. And I still matter."

No one can give you dignity. It was already yours. You may have just forgotten for a while.

Now it is time to remember.

There is something sacred inside you that no circumstance can take away.

Not poverty.

Not addiction.

Not prison time.

Not the opinions of others.

Not even homelessness.

That something is your dignity.

It may be buried under pain. It may be ignored by the world. But it still lives inside you, waiting for you to reclaim it.

Dignity is not pride. It is not ego. It is not pretending everything is okay. Dignity is knowing your life has worth, even when your clothes are worn, your ID is missing, or your last meal was yesterday. It is the quiet belief that *I still matter*, even if no one sees it yet.

Being homeless can feel like being erased. People cross the street when they see you. Cashiers speak down to you. Security guards follow you. Job applications disappear into silence. Even eye contact becomes rare.

That kind of treatment does something to the soul. It can make you start questioning whether you belong anywhere, whether you are even a person in the eyes of others. But the truth is: **you do not need permission to be human.** And you do not need approval to have dignity.

The world does not give you dignity, it only reflects what you believe about yourself. And when the world fails to reflect it, you can still carry it. Quietly. Steadily. Privately. Until the time comes to show it again.

What Dignity Looks Like in Hard Times

It is not about pretending you are not struggling. It is not about being perfect. Dignity shows up in the smallest ways:

- Washing your face in a gas station restroom and looking in the mirror with compassion.
- Saying "thank you" when someone gives, and "no, thank you" when someone disrespects.
- Choosing not to steal, even when it's easy.
- Picking up your trash even if no one else does.
- Standing up straight, even if your shoes are falling apart.

It is doing the next right thing, not to impress others, but because **you are still you**, and you decide how you walk through this.

You Are Not the Labels

People may call you things. Words that stick. Words that burn.

"Junkie."
"Bum."
"Problem."
"Lost cause."

But you are not the words they use. You are not your worst moment. You are not the worst thing you have done, or the worst thing done to you.

You are a person. And even if the world forgot, you can choose to remember.

Reclaiming Starts Inside

You may not be able to change your situation overnight. But you can take back your self-respect, one thought at a time.

- Remind yourself who you once were, and who you still are underneath.
- Treat yourself with care, even if others do not.
- Speak kindly to yourself.
- Carry your story like a traveler, not a failure.

Your story is not over. And as long as you are alive, you have the right to reclaim your place in the world, not just physically, but emotionally and spiritually.

You do not have to wait until you "make it" to reclaim your dignity.

Start now.

Stand up, even if your knees are shaking. Clean your spirit, even if your body is tired. Reclaim your name, your worth, your inner light.

You are still you. You still matter.

This page intentionally left blank for your initial reading reflection

Daily Mindset Tools

Let's start.

How to protect your thoughts when life keeps coming at you? When you are homeless, the battle is not only around you, but also inside you.

The mind gets tired.
The thoughts get loud.
The bad days echo longer than the good.
You start to believe things that are not true, like I am nothing, I will never get out, this is all I will ever be.

But here is the truth: **your mind is a tool, not a trap**, and with care, you can learn to use it in your favor, even in the harshest conditions.

This chapter is about helping you hold on to yourself, one thought at a time.

1. Start the Day with One Positive Sentence

When your first thought of the day is dark, everything else gets colored by it.

So start with just one sentence. Something simple, something real:

- "I'm still here."
- "Today hasn't happened yet."
- "I survived worse."
- "Something good might happen today."
- "I will not talk down to myself today."

Say it out loud. Say it in your head. Say it until it feels a little more true.

2. Use a Reset Phrase

When your thoughts spiral or shame creeps in, use a reset phrase. This is a sentence you say to interrupt the negativity, to reset your emotional state.

Try one of these:

- "That's not me anymore."
- "Let it pass."
- "Breathe. Just breathe."
- "I'm not where I want to be, but I'm not done yet."

You do not need to fight every thought. Sometimes, you just need to redirect.

3. Do not Believe Every Thought You Think

Not every thought in your head is the truth.
Some are echoes from pain.
Some are voices from the past.
Some are just fear trying to protect you from disappointment.

Learn to **question your thoughts**:

- Is this thought helpful or harmful?
- Is it true, or just familiar?

- Would I say this to someone I love?

If the answer is no, let it go.

4. Practice Mental Cleanliness

Just like your body needs a wash, your mind needs one too.
Take 5 minutes each day, morning, noon, or night, to clean your mind.

Here is how:

- Sit still, breathe deep, and release the day.
- Imagine wiping the mental clutter away.
- Say out loud: "I release what's not mine. I release what no longer serves me."

Even one peaceful moment a day is worth it.

5. Create a Personal Power List

Write down 3 to 5 things that give you strength, peace, or direction.

Your list might include:

- A person who believed in you
- A time you overcame something hard
- A song that reminds you of who you are
- A quote, a prayer, or even a memory

When your mind gets noisy, pull out your list and read it like a lifeline.

6. Use This Simple Formula When You are Spiraling:

"What's true + What I can do = My next step."

Example:

- "I feel like a failure." → Truth: I made mistakes, next step: I'm still trying.
- What I can do: Eat something. Walk. Talk to someone. Write. Rest. Read this book.
- That is your next step. Nothing more.

7. End the Day With This Thought

As the night closes in, the mind gets heavy. Before sleep, whether on a bench, a cot, or a floor, say this:

"I made it through. That's enough for today."

Your mind is your shelter, too.

Protect it. Feed it. Speak to it kindly. When the world feels brutal, let your mind be the one place you do not get punished. Every day won't be perfect, but your thoughts do not have to become your enemy. Let them become your strength.

Mental Health While Homeless

There are people out there who want to listen. For real. Not because they feel sorry for you, but because they understand what this kind of life does to a person. There are therapists, caseworkers, hotline responders, street chaplains, nurses, and volunteers who will sit with you and not judge a single thing you say.

You do not have to know where to start.
You just have to be willing to say, "I'm not okay. Can someone help me with this?"

If that is too much, start here. Start now. Say it to me, quietly, in your own heart:
"I do not want to feel like this forever."

That is enough to open a door.

Let me give you a couple of places you can reach out to when you are ready.

Call or text 988 – That Is the Suicide & Crisis Lifeline.

They'll listen. You do not have to be in a crisis to call. They are trained to help people just like you, hurting, confused, tired, or just needing to talk.

There are also **mental health clinics** in many cities that take walk-ins.

Some shelters offer counseling on-site. Ask someone. Do not give up if the first person does not help.

Try again. Because your peace is worth fighting for. And please, if you have ever thought about ending your life, you need to know this:

You are not alone. You are Needed. You still Matter. And this world is not better without you...

You matter. Even like this.
Especially like this.

Take one breath at a time.
Say what hurts.
Let someone hear it.

You do not have to carry all of this by yourself anymore.

I AM NOT ALONE - I STILL MATTER

Because your mind matters, even when your world is falling apart

Being homeless does not just mean losing a home, it often means losing peace of mind. You do not need a diagnosis to know when something is wrong. You feel it. The heaviness. The fear. The anger. The numbness. The confusion.

Some days your thoughts move too fast, other days they won't move at all.
Some nights, sleep won't come.
Other nights, you do not want to wake up.

And through it all, the world expects you to keep surviving like it is easy.

But let us say this out loud: **being homeless is traumatic.** Trauma affects the mind, not just the body.

What You Might Be Feeling, and Why It is Normal

- **Anxiety**, when everything feels uncertain, your body stays in alert mode.

- **Depression**, when nothing seems to improve, you lose the energy to even hope.

- **Rage**, when people treat you as less than human, anger becomes a shield.

- **Shame**, when you feel like a burden, it is easy to believe you do not deserve care.

- **Hopelessness**, when your situation keeps repeating, it is hard to imagine a way out.

- **Disconnection**, when no one looks you in the eye, you start to drift from yourself.

None of these feelings make you weak or crazy. They make you human and hurting.

1. You Are Not "Broken"

Mental health is not about being "crazy."
It's about being overwhelmed by things that would break most people.
Homelessness is not a personal failure; it is a brutal experience that wears down even the strongest minds.

So, instead of calling yourself "crazy," try saying this:
"I am going through something hard, and I deserve support."

That one sentence can begin to change how you see yourself.

2. Look for Safe People to Talk To

You do not have to do this alone. There are people who will listen without judgment.

Places to try:

- **Outreach workers**, many are trained to support mental health, not just offer food or shelter.

- **Local churches or missions,** some offer confidential counseling or prayer support.

- **Health clinics,** even walk-in clinics sometimes have mental health services or referrals.

- **Crisis lines,** they won't judge you, and they're open 24/7.

☏ **National Suicide & Crisis Lifeline: 988 (USA)**
☏ **SAMHSA Helpline: 1-800-662-HELP (4357)**
Free, confidential, and available in multiple languages.

3. Learn the Difference Between Pain and Patterns

Pain is what happened to you.
Patterns are how your mind responds over time.

If you notice yourself stuck in loops, self-blame, paranoia, lashing out, isolating, do not judge it.
Just notice it.
And then ask, "Is there another way I could respond today?"

Sometimes, small mental shifts are the beginning of deep healing.

4. Take One Mental Health Action Per Day

Even one small act of care matters. Try:

- Finding a quiet spot to breathe and release tension.
- Talking to someone who feels safe.
- Writing down what you are feeling, even if you throw the paper away.
- Asking for help, even if it's just directions or support.
- Saying out loud, "I am not my pain."

You do not have to fix everything. You only have to do one thing today that honors your mind.

5. Know This: Suicidal Thoughts Are Not the End

They may feel final. They may feel real. But they are not the truth.

They are your pain screaming to be heard, not a prediction of your future.

If you have had thoughts of ending your life, please know: You are not alone. You are not beyond help. And this is not the end of your story.

Call 988. Or tell someone. Or whisper it to yourself. You matter. You are loved. And you are needed in this world.

Your mental health deserves care, whether you are living in a mansion or under a bridge. Your healing deserves time, whether you have been hurt by others, by yourself, or by a system that failed you. You are still here. And that is the beginning of something.

Addiction and Recovery

If you are struggling with addiction, know I'm not here to blame you, or shame you. I'm not going to tell you to just stop. I am not going to pretend your pain does not have a reason. I am just going to sit with you for a few pages and say this: You are not alone, and you still matter.

Sometimes the only way to survive what you have been through is to numb it. When you do not have a home, a job, or even a safe place to feel pain, substances start to feel like medicine. Or escape. Or maybe the only thing that still gives you a moment of quiet.

Sometimes, the thing that once helped you survive might be the same thing keeping you from moving forward now. You already know that. The question is not whether you are addicted. The question is, are you ready to want something more?

If you are, even just a little, let us talk about what recovery might look like. Not the perfect kind with white rooms and expensive programs. The real kind. The messy kind. The kind that starts right where you are.

Recovery does not mean pretending you are strong. It means letting yourself be human again. It means saying, "This is hard, but I do not want to stay stuck." It means failing sometimes and getting back up anyway. It means letting people help, even when it feels awkward or embarrassing. It means seeing yourself as someone who is worth healing.

Maybe you have tried to quit before. Maybe you have gone through programs, detoxed, relapsed, and said never again, only to find yourself right back where you started. Know this, you did not fail. You are still learning. You still have another chance.

If you want to take one small step toward recovery today, start by speaking this truth out loud, even if it is just to yourself: "I do not want to be ruled by this anymore." That is enough to begin.

There are programs that can help. You do not have to pay for all of them. Many cities have free or sliding scale rehab centers. Some shelters partner with addiction recovery programs. There are also 12-step meetings that do not require anything from you except your honesty. Even if you are not sure you believe in their process, walking into one can be a doorway out of isolation.

But even if you are not ready to walk through any of those doors, there are still things you can do. You can keep this conversation going with yourself. You can choose not to use just for today. Or even just for this hour. You can ask someone how they quit and listen to what they say. You can tell someone you are scared. You can forgive yourself for yesterday and try again tomorrow.

You are not a lost cause. I do not care how many people have told you otherwise. I do not care how long you have used. You are still alive, which means something in you wants to heal. Hold on to that.

Recovery is possible. It does not have to be loud, fast, or pretty. It can be slow. Quiet. Yours.

Staying Safe on the Streets

Surviving the streets is not just about finding food or shelter. It is about staying safe. Safety can feel like a luxury when you are on the streets. Some nights, all you want is to close your eyes without fear. Some mornings, all you want is to know you made it through.

If you have had things stolen, if you have been hurt, harassed, or scared, you are not weak. You are surviving a world that was not built to protect you. That takes strength most people do not understand.

You shouldn't have to live in fight mode all the time. You deserve to feel safe in your body, your space, and your mind. So let's talk about what that can look like, even in a world that does not always make it easy.

First, trust your instincts. If something or someone feels off, listen to that feeling. It is not paranoia, it is survival wisdom. If a place feels wrong, it probably is. If someone's energy makes you uncomfortable, you do not owe them your time, your story, or your space.

Find places that offer you a bit of cover. Public libraries, transit stations during certain hours, church courtyards, daytime shelters, or places where staff or volunteers know you by name. When possible, avoid sleeping fully alone, especially in isolated areas. It may feel like privacy, but it often increases risk. Quiet, semi-visible spots with some foot traffic are often safer.

Hide your valuables well. Even if it is just a phone charger, a bus pass, or a bit of money. Keep small things close to your body when you sleep. Split important items into different places, some in your sock, some in your bag, some hidden in your clothing.

Keep your documents as safe as possible. If you have your ID, social security card, or medical info, treat them like gold. If you lose them, it can be hard to access services or get back on your feet. Some shelters or nonprofits offer lockers or safe storage, use them if you can.

Stay clean, not just for dignity, but for safety. Looking clean and alert, even a little bit, can make you less of a target. Use public restrooms, wipes, or shelter showers when available. It is not about vanity, it is about survival.

Be cautious about who you trust. Yes, there are good people out there. But there are also people who prey on the vulnerable. If someone offers you help and it feels too good to be true, pause. Ask questions. Get space to think.

Watch your energy. You do not need to fight every battle or answer every insult. Some people are hurting and want to spread their pain. Do not carry what is not yours. Protect your peace when you can.

If you are ever in danger or hurt, seek help. There are crisis centers, women's shelters, hotlines, and people trained to protect, not punish, you. You may have been ignored before, but not everyone will turn away.

You are not weak for being careful. You are smart. You are aware. You are still standing.

Safety is not something you should have to fight for, but until the world changes, protect yourself like you matter, because you do.

Faith, Spirituality, or Inner Strength

What you believe in matters. Maybe you pray. Maybe you used to. Maybe you lost your faith somewhere between shelters and sidewalks. Maybe you never had any to begin with. Whatever the case, this chapter is for you. Not to convert you, not to convince you, just to remind you that something greater may still be walking beside you.

When life falls apart, we often look up and ask, why? Why me? Why now? Why does it feel like God, or the universe, or life itself has turned its back? If you have asked those questions, know you are not alone. Many have screamed at the sky in pain. Many have wept in the dark and wondered if anyone, or anything, was listening.

Sometimes, faith feels far away because we think it only lives in churches or books or people who have it all together. But real faith? The kind that keeps you breathing when there's no reason to? It does not need a building. It just needs one quiet whisper inside of you that says, keep going.

Some people call it God. Others call it spirit, light, energy, or the universe, or nothing at all. Whatever you name it, it is still with you. It kept you alive when you did not want to be. It is what helped you find this book, this moment, this page.

Even if you do not believe in anything, maybe believe in this: your ability to keep surviving is sacred. The fact that you have made it through the things you have made it through, that's something holy. That's strength no one can measure.

You do not have to be religious to be spiritual. You do not have to follow rituals or rules to feel connected to something greater. You just have to pause. Breathe. And maybe say something like, "Help me," even if you do not know who or what you are talking to.

If you are someone who believes in God, in prayer, in a divine purpose, do not forget, He has not forgotten you. I know it is hard to believe when your stomach is empty and your feet are blistered, and people look through you like you are not even there. Even in that pain, you are still seen. Still loved. Still held.

Your faith may be battered, but it's not broken. Your spirit may be tired, but it's not lost. And your story is not over.

Try talking to the sky tonight. Or the stars. Or to that part of yourself that still hopes, no matter how quietly. You do not need the perfect words. You just need to show up.

If all you can say is, "Be with me," that is enough.

If all you can feel is, "I'm still here," that is a prayer.

If you cannot feel anything at all, that is okay too. Something greater is still with you, even in silence.

How to Rebuild Relationships

In this chapter, let us talk about people. The ones we loved. The ones we lost. The ones who hurt us. The ones we might have hurt, too.

When you are going through homelessness, relationships get complicated. Sometimes it is the reason you ended up out here. Sometimes it is what fell apart after. Either way, people leave. Or you leave them. Or silence grows so wide between you that it feels impossible to cross.

Maybe you had family that gave up on you. Or friends that stopped calling. Or kids you have not seen in years. Maybe you pushed people away when you were using or angry or ashamed. Maybe you just did not know how to ask for help without feeling small. Whatever the reason, hear this clearly: it is not too late to rebuild.

That does not mean everyone will come back. It does not mean every relationship will be fixed. But healing is still possible, even if all it leads to is peace inside you.

Start with yourself. That may sound strange, but it is real. The first relationship to repair is the one you have with you. The part of you that says, "I deserve love, even now." The part that forgives yourself for what you did not know, or could not do, or could not say in time.

You cannot control how others respond. But you can control how you show up. Maybe one day you write a letter. Or send a message. Or leave a voicemail. Not begging. Not blaming. Just honest.

"Hi. I'm still here. I'm working on myself. I do not expect anything, but I just wanted to say I think of you."

That alone can begin something. If they do not respond? You still showed up. You still tried. That says something about who you are becoming.

If you were hurt by someone, deeply, unfairly, painfully, you do not have to pretend it did not happen. You also do not have to carry that pain forever. Forgiveness is not about saying it was okay. It is about saying you won't let it define you anymore. It is about choosing freedom.

If you hurt someone, and you know it, own it. No excuses. No stories. Just this: "I was wrong. I'm sorry. I'm working on being better." They may not trust you yet. They may not ever. But saying it matters. Because it is part of who you are now.

Sometimes the people you lost are gone forever. Through death, distance, or time. That hurts. But even then, healing is still possible. You can speak to them in your heart. You can say what you never got to say. You can forgive them. Or ask for their forgiveness. You can let go.

Relationships are fragile. They are not impossible. You are not too far gone to love again. Or be loved again. Or simply to feel the warmth of human connection.

You may find new people in your life. A shelter worker who treats you with respect. A fellow survivor who becomes like family. A stranger who sees your worth.

Do not block them out because You are afraid. Let them in slowly. Carefully. But let them in.

Love is risky. But loneliness is brutal. And you were not made to be alone forever.

Start small. Make eye contact. Say thank you. Ask how someone's doing. Share a piece of your story when it feels safe. Bit by bit, bridge by bridge, you rebuild.

No matter what, do not close your heart for good. Keep it cracked open, just enough for light to get in. And for love to find its way back.

This page intentionally left blank for your initial reading reflection

Navigating the System

Dealing with the system can feel like running in circles. One office sends you to another. One worker says one thing, and the next says the opposite.

You wait in lines.

You fill out forms.

You answer personal questions.

And half the time, it feels like no one really sees you.

Here is the truth: as broken as the system can be, it still holds keys. Keys to food, shelter, health care, ID cards, benefits, and a path forward. The trick is learning how to move through it without losing your patience, or your hope.

The first thing you need to know is this: you do not need to have it all together to ask for help. You do not need the right words, the right clothes, or a clean record. You just need to show up, breathe, and speak your truth.

If you have lost your ID, that is usually the first thing to replace. Without it, most services cannot help you. Go to the local DMV, but before you do, ask a shelter, caseworker, or nonprofit if they can help cover the fee or provide documentation. Many can. If you have any old mail, expired ID, jail bracelet, or document with your name on it, bring it.

Social Security cards can be replaced, too. Visit your local Social Security office. If you have had one before, they can look you up. If you have never had one, they'll tell you what you need. Some cities have advocates who will go with you, ask around.

Applying for food stamps, general relief, or disability benefits can take time. But they're lifelines. Go to your local Department of Social Services or Human Services office. Be honest about your situation. You have the right to ask questions and to understand what you are signing.

When it comes to shelters or transitional housing, spots fill up fast. Call early in the morning. Be polite but persistent. Sometimes, it takes showing up in person more than once. That's not fair, but it's real.

Health care is available. Many cities have free clinics. Federally Qualified Health Centers (FQHCs) treat uninsured people. You can walk in. They won't turn you away because you are homeless. If you have mental health needs or addiction issues, ask if they have counselors or support programs. They usually do.

Do not be afraid to ask for a caseworker or advocate. They know how to talk to agencies and cut through red tape. Even if they're busy, stay on their radar. Leave messages. Keep your name fresh in their mind. It helps.

Keep any documents you are given. Even a crumpled piece of paper could be the key to your next step. If you do not have a safe place to store them, ask a shelter or day center if they have storage options. Some libraries even offer lockers for homeless individuals.

If someone talks down to you, take a breath. Do not let their attitude stop you. The system is hard enough, do not let one person's bad day ruin your chances.

You might get told "no" a few times. Do not stop. The next door could open. That one door could lead to your ID, then to your benefits, then to a job program, then to a place of your own. Keep showing up. Keep asking questions. Keep your head up, even if your feet are tired.

I know it is exhausting. But you are not doing this for nothing. You are doing it for your next chapter. For your name. For your dignity. For your future.

Where to Go for Help

You do not have to do this alone. I know it feels that way sometimes, but there are places, real places, that want to help you. Some are stretched thin. Some are imperfect. But they exist. And some of them are waiting for you to walk through the door.

Let's talk about where you can go when you need food, a place to sleep, someone to talk to, or just a place to sit without being moved along.

If you need food, start with food pantries and community kitchens. Many churches, mosques, temples, and local nonprofits serve hot meals throughout the week. You can ask any shelter, outreach worker, or even a librarian to help you find a list of food banks near you. Some food banks also offer hygiene products, pet food, and clothing.

If you need shelter, time matters. Call or visit early in the day if you can. Ask about availability and how intake works. Some require ID, but many will take you first and

help you get what you need later. If one shelter says they're full, ask if they know another one that is not. Shelters often talk to each other.

If you feel unsafe where you are staying or need a place just for women, children, or LGBTQ+ individuals, ask specifically for a safe space. Some places specialize in trauma-informed care. Do not be afraid to say, "I need a place that is safe for someone like me."

If you need a place to clean up, look for day centers, public recreations centers, and nonprofits that offer showers, laundry, and hygiene kits. Some mobile units drive around cities offering those services. Libraries and gyms sometimes let you use the restrooms and charge your phone, especially if you ask respectfully.

If you are dealing with addiction and you are ready for help, start with local rehab centers or 12-step programs. Hospitals and health clinics can refer you. Many programs have waiting lists, but do not let that discourage you. Get your name on every list you can. Something will open up.

If you are struggling with mental health or feeling like you are not safe in your own mind, call a crisis line. You do not have to be on the edge to make the call. Sometimes just talking to someone helps you step back and breathe again.

988 is a free, 24/7 line in the United States. You can call, text, or chat with someone trained to listen. No judgment. No police unless there's danger. Just someone who gets it.

If you are trying to rebuild, ask about transitional housing, job programs, or case management. Many shelters and nonprofits offer more than just a bed. They can help you get ID, apply for benefits, or get into job training. Ask for a case worker. Follow up. Show them you are serious. That alone can open doors.

If you are not sure where to start, visit a public library. I mean that. Most librarians in their hearts want to help you, and they know about local services and can help you find a number, print a form, or point you in the right direction. Best of all, they will treat you like a person.

You can also call 2-1-1 from most phones in the U.S. It is a free number that connects you to local resources, food, shelter, healthcare, legal help, transportation, and more. Just dial, tell them where you are, and ask what is available near you.

Keep a small notebook or folded piece of paper to write down names, phone numbers, and hours of the places you visit. It helps. You cannot remember everything when you are tired or hungry, and having a little list in your pocket gives you something solid to hold on to.

You deserve help, not judgment. You are not asking for favors, you are asking for your chance. A step forward. A hand up. That is not weakness. That is wisdom.

Small Jobs, Big Steps

Let's talk about work. Not the kind with a suit and a salary. The kind that pays a little, helps a lot, and reminds you that you still have something to give.

When you are homeless, finding a full-time job can feel like climbing a mountain with no shoes. You might not have an ID, a phone, clean clothes, or a place to sleep. But that does not mean you cannot earn. It just means you have to start differently.

Small jobs matter. They might not be glamorous. They might not pay much. But they remind you of something important, that you are still capable.

Start with what you know. Can you fix things? Carry things? Watch kids? Clean? Paint? Cook? Sort? Listen? There is someone out there who needs what you know how to do. Your job is to start asking, offering, and showing up.

Go where people need help. Churches, food banks, community centers, flea markets, small stores, landscaping crews, construction sites, and even local restaurants. Ask if they need extra help. Be polite. Be real. Say something like, "I'm looking to earn a little. I can sweep, clean, move, or help however you need."

You would be surprised how many people say yes, not because they pity you, but because they respect your hustle.

If you are near a recycling center, gather cans and bottles. It may not feel like much, but it adds up. If you are near a tourist area, consider offering simple services, like cleaning windshields, holding signs, or even sharing music if you play an instrument. But always check the local laws first to stay out of trouble.

If you are creative, use it. Some people make jewelry or small art pieces and sell them on sidewalks or online with help from libraries. Others write signs with inspiring messages. If you are someone who has a story to tell, people will often give when they feel your heart.

Public libraries often offer job boards, computers, and workshops to help you apply for work. Some even have staff trained to help people rebuild their résumés or practice interviews. Use those tools. They're there for you.

Ask about day labor agencies. Some hire people for one-day jobs, moving furniture, cleaning out garages, helping at events. You do not always need ID. But show up early, dress as clean as you can, and be honest about your availability.

If you qualify for General Relief or EBT, ask if your county offers a work-for-benefits program. Some counties will give you extra benefits or prioritize you for housing if you participate.

Also, if you are at a shelter, ask if they partner with job training programs. Many do, and they're often happy to recommend people who show up and try.

One more thing. No job is beneath you. Do not let pride block your first step. What matters now is not how it looks. It is that it moves you forward. A dollar earned with dignity is better than a hundred received with shame.

Every time you show up, help someone, do your best, you are building trust, skill, and confidence. Those are the foundations of stability. Do not underestimate them.

Your small steps today could become someone's reason to recommend you tomorrow. That could turn into something bigger. Then bigger still. It all counts.

Stories of People Who Made It

Please meet these people. You may never shake their hand or hear their voices, but know they exist. Not as myths, not as perfect success stories, but as reminders. They walked through homelessness, and they made it out.

Some still carry the scars. Some still struggle. But they are not where they used to be. And that means maybe, just maybe, you won't be either.

Let me tell you about Marcus. He lived in his car for almost two years after losing his job in a factory. No savings. No backup. His family was across the country, and pride kept him from calling. Every night, he parked in quiet neighborhoods, hoping not to be noticed. During the day, he showered at the gym and applied for jobs at the library. He got turned down dozens of times. Then one day, someone did not turn him away. They gave him a chance stocking shelves. It was not much, but it gave him a place to start. A few months later, he was renting a room. Now he works full time and mentors other men trying to get back on their feet. He says the hardest part was not the hunger, it was believing he still had value. Once he remembered that, things started to shift.

Then there is Elena. She escaped an abusive relationship with her two kids and nothing but a backpack. They bounced between shelters. She cried in public bathrooms. She felt like a failure. But one day, a women's center offered her a transitional housing program and helped her apply for classes. She started studying nursing, one course at a time. It took her four years. She's now a licensed caregiver, working nights, taking care of people who cannot care for themselves. She says every shift is sacred. Because she knows what it feels like to need someone to show up.

You might not know James. But you have seen someone like him. Addicted for twenty years. In and out of jail. Burned every bridge. Slept in alleys and under bridges. Everyone thought he was gone for good. But in his fifties, after an overdose that nearly killed him, he checked into a rehab center one more time. Something clicked. He stuck with it. Got clean. Stayed clean. Found a community. Now he runs a small recovery group for others who feel like it is too late. He says, "If you are breathing, you have still got a shot."

Let me tell you about Debbie. She was 19 when her parents kicked her out for coming out as queer. She slept in parks, rode buses all night, and tried to disappear. But someone saw her. A librarian who asked if she was okay. That librarian gave her a list of shelters. Debbie found a place that understood what she was going through. They did not try to fix her, they just accepted her. She is now in school studying to become a counselor for LGBTQ+ youth who have been through what she has. She says the moment someone saw her changed everything.

These people are not superheroes. They just did not stop trying. You do not have to follow their path. You will find your own. Maybe slower. Maybe sideways. But still yours.

Let their stories be proof that pain is not the end. That healing is messy, but possible. That no one's story is too far gone to take a new turn.

You do not have to believe in yourself fully today. Just enough to turn the page.

Sometimes, the person who sees you, might actually be you. That is where something powerful begins. Because sometimes you do not find community, you build it.

You can be your own community activist. Even with nothing in your pocket, you still have your voice. You still have your heart. You still have the power to gather others like you, unhoused, overlooked, and human, and remind them they matter too.

Start simple. Talk to the others who sleep near you. Offer to share what little you have. Create a buddy system. Look out for each other. Pick a safe place where a few of you can meet, share info, rotate watch, or trade resources. Set a tone: respect, safety, and no judgment.

If someone knows where free meals are being served, write it down and pass it on. If someone hears about a job opening, share it. If one of you gets housing, help them stay in touch. Do not let each other disappear into isolation.

You do not have to be famous or educated or perfect to lead. You just have to care. When you are homeless, caring about each other is an act of quiet rebellion against the system that keeps you invisible.

Some of the strongest voices in the housing rights movement used to be on the street. They got tired of waiting to be rescued. So, they started organizing. Protesting. Creating encampments with rules, safety, and community. Some created newsletters. Some spoke at city hall. Some just made sure no one in their group went hungry that day.

That can be you too.

Being unhoused does not mean being powerless. It means being part of a truth that the world does not want to face, and that truth can lead to change.

So, while you work to rebuild your own life, think about how you can help rebuild someone else's too. Not because it is your job, but because it reminds you who you are. Strong. Compassionate. Needed.

You can be the person who says to others, "Come sit with us. You belong." You do not just get to survive this. You get to lead through it.

Journaling Pages or Prompts

There are things you have seen that you have never spoken about. Things you have felt that have no words.

This chapter is a quiet space for those things.

Sometimes you do not need advice or answers. You just need somewhere to let your thoughts land. A place that won't talk back or judge or look away. That is what these pages are for.

You do not have to be a writer. You do not even have to spell things right. Just speak to the page like it is someone who truly listens. Let it catch what is been circling in your head.

If you have a pen and something to write on, great. If not, just read the prompts. Let them stir something inside you.

Speak your answers aloud or keep them in your heart. It still counts.

Here are a few to start with:

What is something you wish someone knew about you right now?

What is one memory that reminds you are strong?

What do you want tomorrow to feel like?

Who did you use to be before things got hard?

What part of you has not given up yet?

Write about a time you helped someone else. How did it feel?

Describe what safety would feel like, not just where you would be, but how your body would feel in that space.

If you could speak to your younger self, what would you say?

What are three things you have survived that most people wouldn't understand?

Write a letter to the version of you that makes it out of this. What do you want to tell them?

I AM NOT ALONE - I STILL MATTER

This is not about being poetic or perfect. It is about being honest. Maybe even being kind to yourself for once.

If you do not have paper, say these words aloud. If you do not feel safe speaking them, whisper them inside your mind. They will still be yours.

Every time you tell the truth, to yourself, to the page, to the air, you reclaim a little piece of your voice.

You deserve to be heard.

What to Say to Yourself Every Day

The world might not be kind to you right now. People might ignore you, judge you, or treat you like You are invisible. But there is one voice you hear more than anyone else's, and that is your own.

What you say to yourself matters. Especially when you are tired, hungry, angry, or alone. The way you talk to yourself can either tear you down or keep you going.

You might not be able to control what happens around you. But you can choose what happens inside your mind.

Here are some things to say to yourself. Every day. Or every hour if you need to. Not because they are magic, but because they are true, and because hearing them helps you remember who you are.

I'm still here. And that means I still have a chance.

I am not worthless. I am not my worst moment.

Today does not have to look like yesterday.

I AM NOT ALONE - I STILL MATTER

I do not have to believe every negative thought I have.

I matter, even if no one says it out loud.

I will not talk to myself like I'm nobody. I deserve better.

There is something good in me, even if no one sees it yet.

I've survived this far. That means I know how to survive.

One small step is still a step.

This is not where my story ends.

Some days, all you will be able to say is, "Keep going." That is enough.

If your inner voice is cruel or full of shame, speak back to it. Say, "Not today." Say, "I'm learning a different way." Say, "That's not who I am anymore."

No one taught you how to talk kindly to yourself, especially if you were raised in chaos or grew up feeling like a problem. But you can teach yourself now.

Make up your own phrases. Write them down. Repeat them like a rhythm. Say them until your mind begins to believe you. Say them even when it does not.

Your voice is the one you live with. Make it a voice that helps you heal.

You deserve to be spoken to with respect. Start with you.

A Directory of Love

Sometimes what we need most is proof that the world has not fully forgotten us. That somewhere, someone still cares. Not out of charity. Not out of pity. But out of shared humanity.

This chapter is a directory, not just of resources, but of love. Places, people, and possibilities that exist because someone, somewhere, decided you deserve help.

Let us start with national resources, ones you can reach almost anywhere in the U.S., no matter what state you are in.

Emergency Shelter and Services
📞 2-1-1 (United Way): Just dial 211 from any phone. Tell them your location, and they'll help you find food, shelter, medical help, job programs, and more.
☐ www.211.org

Mental Health and Crisis Support
📞 988 Suicide & Crisis Lifeline: Call or text 988

anytime, day or night. Trained counselors will listen.
☐ www.988lifeline.org

Addiction Help
☎ SAMHSA National Helpline: 1-800-662-HELP (4357) - They offer free, confidential help for mental health and substance use.
☐ www.samhsa.gov

Domestic Violence and Abuse
☎ National Domestic Violence Hotline: 1-800-799-SAFE (7233) or text "START" to 88788
☐ www.thehotline.org

LGBTQ+ Youth and Support
☎ The Trevor Project: 1-866-488-7386 or text "START" to 678678
☐ www.thetrevorproject.org

Veterans in Crisis
☎ Veterans Crisis Line: 1-800-273-8255, press 1 Or text 838255
☐ www.veteranscrisisline.net

Health and Clinics
🔎 Look for Federally Qualified Health Centers (FQHCs)
They provide care even if you do not have insurance.
☐ www.findahealthcenter.hrsa.gov

Food Resources
🔎 Feeding America: Enter your zip code to find local food banks.
☐ www.feedingamerica.org/find-your-local-foodbank

Legal Help
🔎 Legal Aid services exist in most counties to help with housing, benefits, and ID issues.
Check your local library or 211 for contact info.

ID and Social Security Replacement
🔎 Social Security Administration
☐ www.ssa.gov/ssnumber

🔎 DMV (Department of Motor Vehicles)
Every state has its own website. Search for yours with "your state + DMV."

Work and Reentry Support
🔑 Goodwill Industries
They offer job training and help people re-enter the workforce.
☐ www.goodwill.org

🔑 America Works
Helps individuals with barriers to employment find jobs.
☐ www.americaworks.com

Faith-Based and Local Support
Many churches, mosques, synagogues, and temples offer help regardless of your religion. Food. Blankets. A place to sit. Someone to pray with, or just talk to.

Ask them, even if you have never been inside before. You do not have to believe what they believe to be treated with compassion.

Do not forget about the library. It may not seem like much, but it can be everything, a bathroom, computer access, warmth, and most of all, someone who won't look at you like you do not belong.

This is your directory of love. Keep it close. Use it when you feel alone. Let it remind you that not all doors are closed. And not every heart has turned cold.

Help exists. You are allowed to reach for it.

When You Help Some Else You Heal Too

There may come a moment, maybe not today, maybe not tomorrow, when someone who is struggling the way you once did looks at you and asks, "What should I do?"

In that moment, something inside you will rise. Not pride, not ego, but your *purpose in life. Stand up.* Rise and find your purpose in life.

Because even when you did not have a bed, you carried wisdom. Even when you felt worthless, you were learning. Even when you were quiet, your soul was taking notes. One day, someone else will need those notes to survive.

You may not feel like a teacher. You may not feel like a leader. But the moment you offer kindness, truth, or direction to someone who needs it, that is who you become.

If you are sleeping in a shelter tonight and someone new walks in, say hello. If you are in a line for food and see someone scared or lost, tell them where to go. If you have already walked through the worst of it, tell someone else they can make it too.

It might not feel like much. But to them, it could be everything.

Helping does not mean having all the answers. It means being honest. It means being present. It means using what nearly broke you to build something for someone else.

Here is the truth most people do not talk about, when you help someone else, you start to heal too. You remember your strength. You remember your story has meaning. You stop seeing yourself as a problem to fix and start seeing yourself as a light that can guide.

No act of compassion is wasted.

Maybe all you have is a kind word. A piece of bread. A phone number. A few minutes of your time. Offer it. Freely. Without pity. Without preaching. Just human to human.

You do not have to be better than someone else to help them. You just have to care. And you already do. That is why you are still here. That is why you are still reading.

So, wherever you go from here, whether into housing, into healing, or into tomorrow, carry this truth with you:

You have got something to give. And when you give it, the world changes. A little. Quietly. But it changes.

So, go be someone's reminder. Just like this book was yours. Pay It Forward, and it will come back multiple folds.

A Note from Someone Who Cares

If no one has told you lately, let me be the one to say it.

I care. I see you.

Maybe not your face. Maybe not your name. But I see your courage. I see your pain. I see the quiet strength it takes to survive a world that looks through you.

This book was never about fixing you. You are not broken. You are human. And being human means you are allowed to fall apart. You are allowed to struggle. You are allowed to make mistakes and fix them. You are allowed to need help, and rest, and truth.

But it also means this: You are allowed to begin again.

This life has not been fair to you. That is the truth. But your story is still yours. No one else gets to decide how it ends.

I do not know where you will go next. I do not know how long it will take. Just believe in your ability to take

the next right step. Then the one after that. Even if it is slow. Even if it is messy. Even if no one claps for you but you.

You are worth the space you take up.
You are not forgotten.
You are not alone.
You still matter.

If you ever doubt it, come back to this page. Read these words again. Let them find you when you need them most. Because they are not just words. They are a promise from one human being to another:

You were never meant to disappear. Believe in yourself that you can rise and join society again.

About Dr. Abraham Khoureis, Ph.D.

Dr. Abraham Khoureis, Ph.D., was named the Apostle of Compassionate Leadership by his colleagues and leadership professional inner circle. A multi-talented thought leader and partner, author, an award-winning mentor, and advocate for compassionate leadership. He is an adjunct professor who specializes in teaching graduate-level courses in business and management, blending academic theory with real-world business practices.

Dr. Khoureis is also a small business owner and holds numerous state certifications and professional designations and licenses, showcasing his multidisciplinary expertise.

He is the Creator and Developer of the Compassionate Leadership Model and Pyramid, which emphasizes leadership built on self-awareness, mindfulness, and commitment to serving others without expectation of return.

Moreover, Dr. Khoureis developed the Disability Learning Attainment Model, a framework designed to empower individuals with disabilities through inclusive education, skill-building, and leadership development. Through his writing, he advocates and advances positive societal change. His work champions and empowers inclusivity, accessibility, and ethical practices in both education and leadership. He has been published on *Forbes.com*, *Newsweek.com*, and the distinguished *Leader to Leader Journal*. He was recognized as LinkedIn's Top Leadership and Management Voice, and Thinkers 360's Top 50 Voices.

Dr. Abe's contributions extend to his writings, professional leadership development initiatives, and thought leadership, making him a respected emerging leader in the fields of compassionate leadership, organizational behavior, and human development.

Readily available at: DrAbeKhoureis.com
Social Media: @DrAbeKhoureis
DrAbeBooks.com

For his latest published work, also visit Amazon.com Search for Dr. Abraham Khoureis, Ph.D.

Other Books by Dr. Abraham Khoureis, Ph.D.

The Balance In Between: Finding the Balance Between Emotional Intelligence and Emotional Stupidity
ISBN: 979-8-9895211-2-8

Decoding Microaggressions for Leaders and Beyond: Understanding Microaggressions Face-to-Face
ISBN: 979-8-9895211-4-2

Hollywood Dream: How To Make It In Tinseltown
ISBN: 979-8-9895211-7-3

Protect Your Business: Stay Informed, Stay Ahead
ISBN: 978-1-966837-09-1

Reasonable Accommodation: Empowering Inclusion
ISBN: 979-8-9895211-3-5

Revealing the Seven Secrets to Exceptional Mentorship
ISBN: 978-1-966837-00-8

SELF: Introducing The Self Rotating Model
ISBN: 979-8-9895211-5-9

The Compassionate Leadership Model and Pyramid
ISBN: 979-8-9895211-0-4

www.ingramcontent.com/pod-product-compliance
Lightning Source LLC
LaVergne TN
LVHW011428080426
835512LV00005B/329